RHINO RESCUE

RHINO RESCUE

GARRY HAMILTON

FIREFLY BOOKS

A Firefly Book

Published by Firefly Books Ltd. 2006

First printing

PUBLISHER CATALOGUING-IN-PUBLICATION DATA (U.S.)
(Library of Congress Standards)

Hamilton, Garry., 1962–

Rhino rescue : changing the future for endangered wildlife / Garry Hamilton.
[64] p. : col. photos. ;   cm.   (Firefly animal rescue)
Includes index.
Summary: Provides details and facts about rhinoceros from around the world, their endangerment and
a range of conservation programs to save them, including profiles of individual conservationists and rhino species.
ISBN-13: 978-155297-912-9   ISBN-13: 978-155297-910-5
ISBN-10: 1-55297-912-1 (BOUND)   ISBN-10: 1-55297-910-5 (PBK.)

1. Rhinoceroses—Juvenile literature. 2. Endangered species—Juvenile literature.
3. Wildlife conservation—Juvenile literature. I. Title. II. Series.
599.66/8 dc22   QL737.U63H36 2006

LIBRARY AND ARCHIVES CANADA CATALOGUING IN PUBLICATION DATA
Hamilton, Garry, 1962—
Rhino rescue : changing the future for endangered wildlife / Garry Hamilton.
(Firefly animal rescue)
Includes index.
ISBN-13: 978-155297-912-9   ISBN-13: 978-155297-910-5
ISBN-10: 1-55297-912-1 (BOUND)   ISBN-10: 1-55297-910-5 (PBK.)
1. Rhinoceroses—Juvenile literature. 2. Endangered species—Juvenile
literature. 3. Wildlife conservation—Juvenile literature. I. Title. II. Series.
QL737.U63H34 2006   j599.66'8   C2005-904579-5

Published in the United States by
Firefly Books (U.S.) Inc.
P.O. Box 1338, Ellicott Station
Buffalo, New York 14205

Published in Canada by
Firefly Books Ltd.
66 Leek Crescent
Richmond Hill, Ontario L4B 1H1

Cover and interior design by Ingrid Paulson

Printed in China

*The publisher gratefully acknowledges the financial support for our publishing program by the Canada Council for the Arts,
the Ontario Arts Council and the Government of Canada through the Book Publishing Industry Development Program.*

TABLE OF CONTENTS

THE COMEBACK KID

Throughout history, the rhinoceros has been regarded as nature's heavy hitter—a powerful beast that can weigh 3 tons (2,700 kg) while wielding a deadly horn up to 5 feet (1.5 m) long. It's well known for charging humans, head-butting trees, buckling the sides of rugged vehicles and stomping its way through roaring campfires.

Now the rhino has a new reputation—the comeback kid.

Ruthlessly slaughtered for centuries, these great beasts are one of conservation's great success stories. Just look at the white rhinoceros, the second-largest land mammal next to the African elephant. A century ago there were only a few dozen living in a single game reserve in what is now South Africa. Today there are nearly 12,000 in several African countries, and the number continues to grow each year.

Or consider the Indian rhino of central Asia. In India's Kaziranga National Park this species numbered barely a dozen in the early 1990s. Now there are 1,550 of these magnificent animals. In Nepal too, the Indian rhino is being reintroduced into its former range.

Even the notoriously aggressive black rhino, victim of one of the worst wildlife massacres ever, appears to be making a comeback.

The story is not all brightness. The total number of rhinos alive today—estimated at 17,500—remains only a fraction of what it was even 30 years ago. And both the Javan and Sumatran rhinos of Southeast Asia remain perilously close to extinction. Poaching (illegal hunting) remains a constant threat as demand for rhino horn remains high, both as a traditional Asian medicine, and to make ceremonial dagger handles that are highly treasured by Muslims in Yemen.

But conservation efforts around the world are addressing these problems, and the rising numbers suggest there's good reason for optimism. For now at least, the brute is back.

WHERE DO RHINOS LIVE?

Five species of rhino
live in Africa and Asia:

White rhinos *(Ceratotherium simum)* –
about 11,640 mainly in South Africa.

Black rhinos *(Diceros bicornis)* –
about 3,100 in South Africa, Namibia and Zimbabwe.

Indian rhinos *(Rhinoceros unicornis)* –
about 2,400 in India and Nepal.

Sumatran rhinos *(Dicerorhinus sumatrensis)* –
about 300 in Indonesia and Malaysia.

Javan rhinos *(Rhinoceros sondaicus)* –
about 60 in the Indonesian island of Java.

THE STORY SO FAR

Humans have been concerned about the fate of the rhinoceros for more than a century. The massive slaughter of white rhinos by Europeans in southern Africa during the 19th century almost wiped out the animal, but early conservation efforts were surprisingly successful.

∧ When Europeans came to Africa in the 19th century, white rhino were slaughtered en masse.

By the early 1960s, when the white rhino was already recovering, the other four species began to face new threats: growing human populations in Asia, more guns in Africa, and the skyrocketing price of rhino horn, which encouraged hunters to kill rhinos for profit.

Today, three subspecies are close to extinction. For the most part, however, there is optimism for the others.

1895: The government of Natal (now South Africa) establishes a protected zone for white rhinos, known today as Hluhluwe-Umfolozi Park.

1908: India establishes Kaziranga National Park to help protect the Indian rhino.

1961: South Africa's Operation Rhino begins moving white rhinos from Hluhluwe-Umfolozi to other areas where the species once lived.

1968: South Africa allows the limited sport hunting of white rhinos, a controversial move that during the next three decades raises US$24 million for rhino conservation.

1975–1977: All rhino species are protected by the Convention on International Trade in Endangered Species (CITES), which bans most international trade in animal parts such as horns.

Two white rhinos amble through the acacia-tree-dotted plains of Hluhluwe-Umfolozi Park, ground zero for the species' remarkable recovery.

1984: Zimbabwe responds to the slaughter of its black rhinos with Operation Stronghold, a shoot-to-kill policy that will lead to the deaths of 178 suspected poachers.

1988: A second population of the rare Javan rhino is discovered in Vietnam.

1989: South African national parks begin auctioning white rhinos at market value, raising millions of dollars for conservation.

1996: The United States passes the Rhinoceros and Tiger Conservation Act, which provides yearly money for rhino conservation projects in Asia and Africa.

1997: Yemen agrees to join CITES and stop trading rhino horns, but it is criticized for breaking the rules. In 2002, the prime minister vows to keep the country's promise.

2001: Andalas, the first captive-bred Sumatran rhino in 112 years, is born on September 13 at the Cincinnati Zoo.

2003: World Wildlife Fund (WWF), along with national parks in South Africa, launches the Black Rhino Range Expansion Project, a three-year effort aimed at encouraging the breeding of rhinos by private landowners.

THE 5,000-POUND VEGETARIAN

Until around 11,000 years ago, Earth was dominated by "megaherbivores"—extra-large animals that ate only plants. Of these oversized vegetarians, rhinos are one of the last surviving groups. Not surprisingly, today's five living species of rhinos have voracious appetites. And knowing their dietary needs is an essential part of conservation.

The white rhinoceros is purely a grazer, eating almost nothing but short grass, and it's well built for the task. The white rhino's extra-long skull—moved by a mass of ligament and muscle that gives it its hunchback appearance—allows it to walk with its head at ground level. Its flat, wide upper lip is perfect for gripping an 8-inch (20 cm) swath of grass. It's also got a mouth full of giant molars shaped just right for grinding tough fibers into a more easily digestible pulp.

If the white rhino is nature's lawnmower, the black rhino is its shrub shears. This species spends its time eating leaves, twigs and bark from bushes and small trees, as well as ripping saplings right from the ground. Scientists call them browsers. To help with their dining, black rhinos have what's known as a prehensile upper lip—a short, trunk-like appendage that can be used for gripping branches.

The Indian rhino is primarily a grazer, but it also feeds on vegetation found near large rivers. These include giant elephant grasses that can grow 26 feet (8 m) high, as well as leaves and fruit from nearby forests. It will also immerse itself in water to feed on the lush aquatic grasses found in marshy areas, submerging its entire head to rip these plants up by their roots.

The Sumatran and Javan rhinos are both browsers adapted for life in the rainforest. One recent study found that Javan rhinos eat the fruit, leaves, twigs, bark and saplings of no fewer than 183 different plants.

Protected by a seemingly impenetrable hide, a black rhino relishes a lunch of needle-sharp thorns.   >

ONE PREDATOR TOO MANY

R hinos are good at defending themselves. They can use their enormous size and aggressive nature to intimidate even tigers and lions. A keen sense of smell helps them detect danger at a distance. Nature has even equipped them with their own private alarm system—oxpeckers. These sharp-eyed birds ride around on rhinos' backs, eating ticks and raising a ruckus whenever there's a stir.

But rhinos are no match for humans.

Cave paintings show that early humans have been hunting rhinos for thousands of years. In the 1800s, however, European hunters moved in waves across southern Africa, slaughtering the white rhino for sport, and to clear land for settlement. By 1890, the formerly wide-ranging animal was on the verge of extinction.

Humans have also slaughtered rhinos (particularly black rhinos) for their horns. They dug pit-traps, laced rhino habitat with electrified trip wire, set leg snares, filled pumpkins and oranges with poison and gunned down rhinos from jeeps using powerful rifles. They removed the horns with chainsaws and then left the bodies to rot.

∧ Born with the misfortune of possessing a valuable horn, the rhino is easy prey for chainsaw-wielding poachers.

When people and rhinos compete for the same land, the animals are treated like any other pest. As a result, all three Asian species have been eliminated from most of their former ranges during the past century.

Today, a few old male white rhinos are still hunted legally in South Africa for a fee that is often channeled back into rhino conservation. Poaching, meanwhile, remains a major threat, and it's kept under control only by around-the-clock protection from highly trained anti-poaching patrols.

< With its nervous oxpecker on the lookout for danger—not to mention ticks—a wide-eared white rhino gets down to the business of grazing.

In 1894, a group of hunters shot six white rhinos in a remote corner of what is today South Africa. It was a despicable deed. The white rhino, symbol of the African savanna, had already been brutally slaughtered for decades. Prior to the hunting party's discovery, the species was already believed to be extinct.

∧ As the king of rhinos, the white rhino is for the most part a gentle giant.

Fortunately there was an outcry, and the land where the shootings occurred was quickly declared a game preserve that is known today as Hluhluwe-Umfolozi Park (the first name is pronounced *shloo-shloowee*). Few could have imagined what happened next. Protected from hunters, the park's 20 to 50 surviving rhinos thrived. By 1960, there were so many that wildlife authorities began transferring them to other areas where they had been wiped out. The official estimate today is 11,640. It's a turnaround that makes the white rhino one of the world's great conservation successes.

White rhinos clearly do well when given a chance. This is partly because they are less aggressive and more tolerant of other rhinos. "White rhinos are really easy animals to conserve," says Martin Brooks, chair of the World Conservation Union's African Rhino Specialist Group. "They're not sensitive, like pandas. You put them in suitable grassland in a suitable climate and they do the rest."

That said, bringing the species back has involved a lot of sweat and tears. In the early days, game wardens at Hluhluwe-Umfolozi had to learn how to sedate the animals—which meant figuring out what drugs to use, and in what doses—and how to transfer the rhinos safely to their new homes. Many rhinos were accidentally killed, and many rangers found out the hard way that, despite the white rhino's gentle reputation, it's still several thousand pounds of wild animal.

Wisely exercising caution, a game warden moves in to hood a partially sedated white rhino in preparation for the animal's capture.

Even after they mastered the art of moving rhinos, there were other painful lessons to be learned. In 1972, the wardens sent 83 white rhinos to neighboring Mozambique, where the species had been extinct since the late 1800s. Unfortunately, poachers began killing them one by one. By 1987, every last reintroduced rhino was dead.

Conservationists learned that it's unwise to reintroduce white rhinos into vast wilderness areas where they can't easily be guarded. Rhino reintroduction programs now focus on smaller game reserves or national parks that can be ringed with miles of electrified fences and patrolled by armed guards on the lookout for poachers. This tough approach has worked: several reintroduced populations are growing so fast that they're producing export rhinos of their own.

A small battalion of game wardens—keenly aware of the danger at hand—readies a full-grown white rhino for transport.

Hluhluwe-Umfolozi remains the heart of the recovery. Every southern white rhino alive today is a descendent of the tiny population that lived on this 250,000-acre (1,000 km²) park when it was formed over a century ago. More than 4,000 rhinos have been moved to other areas, and the number rises each year.

Martin Brooks says the recovery has been so successful because conservationists have paid close attention to the relationship between rhinos and their environment. For example, white rhinos prefer grasslands in the low-lying areas near rivers. When food becomes scarce, such as during droughts or when the population expands, animals will move into less suitable areas. In Hluhluwe-Umfolozi, rangers have kept an eye on these overflow areas—when rhinos begin showing up there, it means the population is getting too large. "Every year we go in and skim off the excess rhinos from those areas," says Brooks. "Some years it might be 30, some years it could be 80 or more." These rhinos are then moved to other areas.

Ironically, now the challenge for conservationists in South Africa is what to do as the white rhino population continues to grow. With poaching still a major threat, reintroducing them to large unfenced reserves remains out of the question. The protected areas, meanwhile, are gradually running out of room.

One option is convincing local communities that devoting land to preserving white rhinos and other animals can be a way to make money. "We want all the people in this country to appreciate the wildlife we have," says Brooks. "And we want them to be able to use it for their benefit. That's the big challenge now."

∧ Out like a two-ton sack of potatoes, a fully sedated white rhino is one bumpy ride away from a life safe from poachers.

Esmond Martin didn't know what to expect the day he met Sheikh Ahmed Zabarah, the Grand Mufti of Yemen. The year was 1991, and Martin was in the Middle Eastern country trying to stop the use of rhino horn in the making of ceremonial dagger handles, a centuries-old Islamic tradition that has contributed greatly to the decline of rhinos in Africa. The Grand Mufti, Yemen's supreme religious leader, was the perfect person to help. But would he listen?

∧ Esmond Martin (left) enlisted the support of religious leader, Sheikh Zhmed Zabarah to help prevent the killing of rhinos.

As it turned out, the Grand Mufti offered to issue a religious decree stating that killing rhinos was against God's will. "He understood the situation very well," recalls Martin. "And that was very encouraging."

As one of the world's leading rhino conservationists, Martin has spent 25 years trying to stop the rhino horn trade, both in Yemen and throughout Asia, where powdered horn is used in traditional medicines. It's an unusual and sometimes dangerous career that he stumbled upon by accident. Born and raised in the United States, Martin came to Kenya in 1964 to work as a geographer. While researching trade patterns along the east coast of Africa, he learned that rhino horns were being shipped to Yemen in large quantities, a discovery that got him interested in conservation. In 1978, he conducted the first investigation into the international rhino horn trade.

Martin discovered that rhino horn was used in traditional Asian medicines to reduce fever. He also found that Yemen, not China, was the main rhino horn market at the time. More and more Yemeni men, with new jobs created by the Middle East oil boom, could now afford daggers with prestigious rhino horn handles. At least 6,600 pounds (3,000 kg) of rhino horn—the equivalent of 1,000 rhinos—were being imported each year.

Rhino horn has long been the most sought-after material for ceremonial dagger handles, such as these being carved in a road-side shop in Yemen.

Martin has traveled to every Asian country where traditional medicines are sold, set up programs to educate people about the plight of the rhinos and promoted alternatives such as buffalo horn for dagger handles and plant extracts for medicines. He hopes new generations will realize there are equally effective, not to mention cheaper, methods for reducing fever.

His efforts are paying off. During his most recent trip to Yemen in 2003, Martin estimated that the country imported less than 65 pounds (30 kg) of rhino horn that year, a 99 percent decline from 1979. But his work continues. "We turned a corner in the early 1990s," he says. "Now we've got to remain vigilant."

FOR THE LUST OF HORN

Scientists have found fossils from rhino-like mammals dating back 50 million years. Most of these ancestors—including one that was 30 feet (9 m) long—lacked what rhinos are now most famous for: their trademark horns.

These impressive weapons vary greatly in size, from the barely detectable nub of the female Javan rhino to the massive front horn of the male white rhino—the largest ever recorded measured in at more than 5 feet (1.5 m) long. African rhinos use their horns for protection against predators, and in fights between males over territory and mates. However, in the early 1990s, the government of Zimbabwe began sawing the horns off its rhinos to protect them from poachers and the animals appeared to survive well without them.

Unfortunately the rhino's pride is much coveted by humans. In traditional Chinese medicine, people have used rhino horn for more than a thousand years, mainly to reduce fever. During the 1800s, Europeans carved door handles and other objects from rhino horn. And in Yemen, ceremonial daggers with rhino-horn handles have long been treasured.

Rhino horn is not made from ivory or bone. Instead it is highly compressed keratin—the same material found in hair and fingernails.

Recently scientists discovered that a rhino's diet can influence the chemical makeup of its horn, giving it a unique "fingerprint." Law enforcement officers hope this will one day help them identify where seized horns originated—evidence that will help bring poachers to justice.

∧ Powdered horn highlights the ingredient lists of scores of traditional Chinese medicines.

< With its unusual profile, a deliberately dehorned white rhino stands a better chance of being ignored by poachers.

WHEN GIANTS COLLIDE

White rhinos sometimes fight over territory or mates. So when game wardens at South Africa's Pilanesberg National Park began finding them dead in 1992, it didn't seem unusual. But then autopsies showed the rhinos were indeed being stabbed, but the wounds were too large and too deep to have been caused by rhino horns. This pointed to another suspect—elephants.

This didn't seem to make sense. African elephants and white rhinos are the two largest land mammals. For thousands of years these giants have worked out ways to live with one another, even if they don't really get along. When they meet at watering holes, for instance, they can confront each other with aggressive acts like foot stomping and ear waving. But one animal usually backs down—and not always the smaller rhino. "Sometimes it depends on who's just finished drinking and who's thirsty," says Rob Slotow, an expert in animal behavior at the University of Natal in Durban, South Africa.

In Pilanesberg, however, the elephants showed no mercy, even when the rhinos backed down. They chased their hapless opponents, sometimes for miles. And given the opportunity, they gored them to death. By 1998, elephant attacks had left 49 white rhinos dead. "That's just not natural," says Slotow.

Eventually scientists were able to solve the mystery. The key was an aggressive hormone-driven state known as musth, which bull elephants enter into when they reach sexual maturity around age 18. Normally these excitable males are kept under control by older, more experienced bulls. In Pilanesberg, however, all the elephants were young, orphaned animals who had been introduced there from another area in the 1980s. When they eventually reached sexual maturity, there were no older males to keep them in check.

Once the scientists realized this, they introduced older elephants into Pilanesberg. The strategy seems to have worked. Since 1998, not a single rhino has been killed by elephants.

< With earth-trembling force, an elephant and a rhino spar over access to precious water.

It was a partly cloudy morning in May 2003, when a Hercules transport plane landed on an unpaved airstrip in the middle of Zambia's North Luangwa National Park. The aircraft had just completed a 3½-hour flight from South Africa with a highly unusual cargo: five black rhinos.

∧ All hooves and ears, a newborn black rhino gives his young legs a test run.

The animals were unloaded and driven to special holding pens known as bomas, where they were kept for several weeks. Each rhino was sedated and fitted with a radio transmitter—inserted into a hole that had been drilled in its horn—so rangers could track their every move once they were let loose into a 21-square-mile (55 km²) fenced area of the park. When this finally happened, the rhinos became the first of their kind in Zambia in almost a decade.

The North Luangwa project, scheduled to involve another 15 rhinos, is just one bit of good news for the black rhino, of which only 3,400 remain in the wild. Uganda and Malawi, two other countries where the species had been eliminated, also have similar schemes underway. Meanwhile, populations in South Africa, Namibia, Zimbabwe and Kenya continue to grow, raising hopes that one of conservation's worst nightmares may finally be over.

Ironically, this species was for a long time the most successful of the world's living rhinos, with a range that stretched over roughly half the African continent. "We think there could have been as many as 850,000 black rhinos in Africa two or three centuries ago," says Richard Emslie of South Africa, chief scientist for the World Conservation Union's African Rhino Specialist Group. "Even by 1960, there were probably 100,000 or so left."

A black rhino keeps its notorious temper in check—at least, for now.

All this changed in the 1970s, largely because of two trends: the rising value of rhino horn, and the spread of high-powered rifles. Between 1970 and 1992, the black rhino population plunged from 65,000 to 2,400. One of the four subspecies, the western black rhino, was nearly eliminated.

Despite its size, the black rhino can run as fast as 35 mph (55kph).

In several countries, such as Zambia, the animals were completely wiped out before anyone could take effective measures. Elsewhere, governments and conservation groups launched massive campaigns to stop the slaughter. Zimbabwe was a prime example. In 1984, it launched Operation Stronghold, a drastic approach that allowed park rangers to shoot poachers on sight. Over the next 10 years, 178 suspected poachers and four game wardens were killed.

When even this failed, conservationists realized that nothing could save black rhinos as long as they were running loose in areas too large to protect. As a result, Zimbabwe began rounding up its remaining rhinos in the early 1990s. Some were transferred to large fenced-in areas, while others were shipped to oversees zoos for captive breeding programs. Officials even convinced cattle ranchers to combine their properties into game reserves. As a result, Zimbabwe was able to keep its black rhinos from being wiped out. This, plus similar work in South Africa, Namibia and Kenya helped stabilize the populations of three out of the four black rhino subspecies. After bottoming out between 1992 and 1995, the numbers have risen by more than 25 percent.

> But Emslie cautions that the species isn't yet in the clear. "People are wary that if the guard is relaxed, then very quickly the wheels can fall off. And history has shown that can happen."

Fortunately, conservationists aren't relaxing. One new effort is South Africa's Black Rhino Range Expansion Project. The goal is to encourage landowners to establish game reserves, similar to those that have been so successful in Zimbabwe. These landowners will be loaned black rhinos and given ownership of 50 percent of whatever offspring are produced. Since black rhinos have fetched over US$65,000 each at game auctions, conservationists are hoping this will be an offer too tempting to turn down. If they're right, the black rhino's comeback may have only just begun.

∧ Orphaned rhino calves receive careful attention from a concerned friend.

TURF WARS

Rhinos aren't like herd animals that graze an area bare and then move on. Nor are they like elephants, which often go exploring for new territory. Instead, they remain in small areas and jealously guard their home turf— even if it means battling another rhino to the death.

Rhinos have a carefully established social structure that varies depending on the species and the habitat. Females are usually more social than males, sometimes forming small herds of young adults and other females. Indian rhinos and white rhinos are particularly friendly this way, sometimes hanging out in groups of 20 or more.

Males, on the other hand, are highly territorial. They rule over a patch of land that also differs in size depending on the species and the habitat. Home ranges for male black rhinos, for instance, can vary from little more than one square mile (3 km²) under ideal conditions to 35 square miles (90 km²) in drier areas.

Rhinos depend heavily on scent to mark their territory, kicking around dung, spraying urine and rubbing their horns against trees. Indian and Javan rhinos also leave secretions on the ground using glands on the backs of their feet. The stale water from wallowing holes is another aroma that can be used to mark bushes.

Animals with neighboring home ranges become familiar with one another and rarely fight, even though their territories sometimes overlap. Things can heat up, however, when males decide to try to supplant others, or when a strange rhino appears. This can lead to savage encounters that last for hours.

Conservationists have learned to respect the rhino's territorial needs. When black rhinos are relocated, for example, they are all released at about the same time. This prevents early arrivals from establishing territory and attacking those released later. In addition, conservationists now carefully analyze new habitat to ensure it can comfortably support at least 100 animals. When they feel at home, rhinos are usually eager to thrive.

< Looking like true heavyweights, a pair of rhinos go horn-to-horn amid a growing swirl of dust.

Rob Brett has seen a lot in 20 years of moving rhinos. He's watched a drugged rhino run straight off a cliff. He's seen a pilot put his aircraft into a spin while tracking a speeding rhino. He's watched a winch give out just as it was pulling an 800-kilogram rhino up a ramp onto the back of a truck. But the mere sight of the animal still fills him with awe.

"Whenever you touch a wild rhino when it's lying on the ground, it's always interesting," he says. "It's covered with ticks. It's got an amazing smell. The feet are covered with thorn holes. It really makes you think you're touching a dinosaur."

"Whenever you touch a wild rhino, it really makes you think you're touching a dinosaur."

Brett works in Zimbabwe with the Southern Africa Regional Development Community, where a big part of his job is to oversee rhino reintroduction programs for countries where rhinos have been eliminated due to poaching. Before this he spent several years in Kenya, where he helped move rhinos from heavily poached areas to places where they could be protected. All told, he's been in on the capture and transfer of some 200 rhinos, and he's impressed by how the methods have improved over the years.

When he started his career, tranquilizer drugs took up to 10 minutes to take effect, which meant there was still plenty of time for the rhino to do something dangerous—like run over a cliff. Once the animal was unconscious, there was also the challenge of maneuvering it onto a sled and then cranking it up onto the bed of a truck. This was also a dangerous time for the unconscious rhino. "The rhino's a heavy animal," says Brett. "If it's sitting down or lying down in the wrong position, this can cause paralysis and sometimes serious muscle damage."

Transporting rhinos to new territory has been a key to the animals' comeback.

Today, new drugs only partially sedate an animal, which allows the capture team to direct it safely into a crate, which is then moved with hydraulic cranes. Finally, military transport planes are often used when rhinos are being transported long distances. "The whole idea is to get the animal back up on its feet as soon as possible, to do everything you can to minimize the stress of capture."

As a result, relocations, which have played a key role in rhino conservation since the early 1960s, now take place with far fewer problems. "In the old days, about 10 percent of rhinos died during the transfer, sometimes more," says Brett. "Now it's rare for a rhino to die during capture."

WHAT'S A RHINO WORTH?

In June 2001, 2,000 people gathered in South Africa for an auction of wild animals including six black rhinos. When the bidding was over, a local rancher bought the six rhinos for 3.3 million South African rand (US$410,000). At more than US$68,000 per rhino, it was an auction record that still stands today.

How is it that endangered black rhinos can be bought and sold like racehorses? For one thing, it's perfectly legal. And many conservationists in Africa think it's one of the best hopes for the rhino's long-term survival.

The idea is that if you make a living rhino worth more than a dead one, people are more likely to protect them. So far it's working. An increasing number of game reserves use rhinos to lure sightseers, and in some cases even sport hunters. These reserves are usually well managed by owners keen on building healthy populations. Indeed, since black rhino poaching slowed in the mid-1990s, privately owned populations have increased faster than those on government land.

Many of the rhinos put up for auction come from game reserves where overcrowding is actually a problem. Game officials initially tried giving them away to private landowners. But the landowners did not use the animals to start new populations, preferring instead to turn a quick profit by allowing them to be hunted. Beginning in 1989, auctions changed all this. Not only did they force buyers to treat the rhinos with more respect, but they also generated huge sums of money to help offset the high cost of rhino conservation.

The rhino ranching industry has also led to public demands for governments to crack down on those who kill rhinos illegally. In South Africa, this has already led to stiffer penalties for poachers—something that will benefit all rhinos, privately owned or not.

Wildlife auctions, where animals are bought and sold like rare paintings, are playing an increasingly > vital role in African rhino conservation.

ON THE FRONTLINES | INDIAN RHINOS

I n 1994, villagers living near Nepal's Royal Chitwan National Park volunteered to dig a series of wallowing holes for the park's Indian rhinos, which rely on such locations to escape the heat of the midday sun. The project was not a selfless act—the villagers hoped the rhinos would attract tourists. But conservationists didn't mind. On the contrary, this is just the kind of local involvement needed to ensure the long-term survival of Asia's largest rhino—another species that has made a remarkable comeback.

∧ Game wardens assess the latest strike by poachers.

The Indian rhino once ruled over a territory that stretched from Pakistan to the eastern Indian province of Assam. Centuries ago they were tamed and ridden into battle by Indian armies. But like their cousins in Africa, one-horned rhinos were heavily hunted during the 19th and 20th centuries, both for sport and for their horns. An additional menace emerged in the 1950s, when humans began using pesticides to wipe out malaria-carrying mosquitoes in river valleys that had once been uninhabitable because of disease. With this new land opened to settlement, humans pushed the rhinos out of their habitat, and by the early 1970s, the entire population was barely 1,000 animals.

Looking like an armour-plated prehistoric beast, an Indian rhino lords over a sea of lush grasses.

Fortunately, people had already taken measures to protect the species. Kaziranga National Park, in the center of Assam, was formed in 1908, when there were thought to be no more than a dozen rhinos living there. But thanks to decades of hard work, Kaziranga now has about 1,550 rhinos. Meanwhile in Nepal, roughly 100 rhinos in Chitwan were put under the careful guard of the army in 1976. By 2000, the population had increased to around 550.

Now conservationists want to bring the species back on an even grander scale. Since 1986, 77 surplus rhinos have been captured in Chitwan and moved some 250 miles (400 km) to Royal Bardia National Park. There they've formed the core of Nepal's second major rhino population, which has grown to 100 animals. Conservationists are trying to establish at least 10 different populations with 100 or more animals, which will make the species healthier and less vulnerable than if the animals were packed into just two locations. "You don't want all your eggs in one basket," says Eric Dinerstein, a conservation biologist with WWF who began working with rhinos in Nepal in 1984.

"You want the population to get behind what you're doing."

But humans and rhinos continue to compete for land. By the 1990s, poor farmers were beginning to clear land right up to the borders of Nepal's national parks. This resulted in loss of habitat for the rhinos, and anger from humans as rhinos began wandering into their crops, occasionally injuring or even killing people. The farmers, then, were rarely interested in preserving habitat for rhinos. "When you have that many people living around the reserve, you need local support," says Dinerstein. "You want the population to get behind what you're doing."

Two important laws passed by Nepal in the early 1990s provided help. One declared that up to half of the money collected by national parks was to go back to local communities. The other gave villages the rights to forests surrounding the parks, as long as the people didn't harm the environment. Since then, WWF has helped dozens of communities surrounding Chitwan set up tourism businesses that earn money while at the same time protecting habitat for rhinos.

From the safety of an elephant's back, awe-struck tourists get a close-up view of the Indian rhino's grassy world.

Unfortunately, since 2000 Nepal has been wracked by civil war that has left few soldiers available for rhino protection. As a result, the country lost 30 percent of its rhino population between 2000 and 2005, mostly due to poaching. Fortunately, conservationists like Dinerstein haven't lost hope. "No matter who is in power, everybody is in favor of greater local control and greater community support for conservation. The question now is how far can the benefits go."

39

As one of India's leading rhino conservationists, Bibhab Talukdar often finds himself close to these intimidating animals—sometimes too close. One January morning back in 1998, Talukdar was riding a jeep through Kaziranga National Park when he came upon a female rhino and her one-month-old calf. The animal charged, forcing him into a high-speed retreat that lasted 15 minutes. At one point the rhino was only a few feet away. "I don't know how I was able to save myself that day," he says.

∧ Bibhab Talukdar is one reason rhino conservation in India is on solid ground.

Despite such moments, Talukdar remains a tireless protector of rhinos. In 1989, he helped found Aaranyak, a conservation organization in the northeast Indian state of Assam, home to most of the remaining one-horned rhinos. With this group, Talukdar has tried to convince politicians and the public about the need to protect rhinos and their habitat. He's trained teachers and forest guards, and he's traveled around the world giving presentations about conservation in India.

Talukdar has also been a leader in the struggle to stop poaching. He's the head of Aaranyak's Rhino Conservation Programme, which is supplying radios, solar panels and other equipment to rangers in under-funded national parks and wildlife sanctuaries. It is also providing rangers with ideas on how to nab poachers—a difficult task, since many of them are violent.

Talukdar has even participated in criminal investigations, sometimes assisting police officers, and sometimes working undercover — he's traveled throughout Asia pretending to be both a buyer and a seller of rhino horns. In one recent case, he helped police confiscate a pair of rhino horns and arrest a suspected poacher just a day after two rhinos were killed.

India's Kaziranga National Park has become a popular destination for witnessing the revival of the Indian rhino.

His efforts appear to be paying off. Poaching, which was out of control throughout Assam during the 1990s, has been considerably reduced since 2001. "The morale of the forest staff has been strengthened," says Talukdar.

Having recently completed his PhD, Talukdar could be working at a job that offers more money and less danger. But knowing that he's helping keep one of Earth's most charismatic creatures from going extinct provides even greater rewards. "Being able to contribute to rhino conservation gives me full satisfaction."

ROOM TO ROAM

Rhinos need surprisingly little space—sometimes they're happy to spend their entire lives on a few square miles of habitat. But their needs can still be quite complex.

Consider the rhinos of India. The species spends much of the year living near large rivers, feasting on new grasses that grow in the silt deposited during annual floods. During the floods themselves, the animals retreat to higher forests. In recent years, however, humans near Kaziranga National Park have made getting to those forests more difficult. During severe flooding in 1998, 39 rhinos drowned.

Black rhinos also have specific habitat needs. Conservationists learned this in the 1960s, when the species' numbers in South Africa began to decline sharply. It turned out the problem was years of fire prevention and the disappearance of elephants. Both fire and elephants help prevent the growth of tall, broad-leaved trees that produce too much shade for the plants preferred by the rhinos.

Conservationists rely heavily on their knowledge of the relationship between rhinos and their land. In India, elevated platforms have helped protect one-horned rhinos during floods. In South Africa, the return of natural fire cycles and elephants has improved black rhino habitat.

A bigger challenge is how to stop the ongoing destruction of rhino habitat by humans, a problem that is particularly severe in Indonesia, where illegal coffee plantations are closing in on the highly threatened Sumatran rhino. When resources grow scarce, these rhinos will encroach on crops, making them an easy target for poachers. Conservationists are trying to deal with these problems through community projects that help locals protect themselves and their crops with fences and trenches, and by showing them how to use rhino habitat without destroying it. In this way, rhinos and humans can live together.

< With higher-level land being gobbled up by human development, Indian rhinos increasingly find themselves trapped in flood-prone habitat with nowhere to run.

ON THE FRONTLINES | SUMATRAN RHINOS

For Indonesia's Rhino Protection Units, some days are worse than others. One of the bad days came in October 2001, when one unit found itself face to face with 10 heavily armed poachers. When the confrontation was over, one patrol member had been shot in the leg.

Another low point came in April of the previous year, when a second unit came upon a full-grown Sumatran rhino caught in a leg snare. The men watched helplessly as the animal, badly dehydrated and stressed, died soon after being freed.

∧ A pile of steel traps and snares dramatically illustrates the threat facing Sumatran rhinos.

But the patrol members face such challenges knowing they're all that stands between survival and extinction for one of the world's rarest mammals.

As the smallest living rhino, the Sumatran species has long been a curiosity among scientists. Its folds of thick skin give it an armored, prehistoric look. Its unusually thick hairs are a reminder of its ancestor, the woolly rhinoceros, a beast that roamed the plains of Europe and Asia during the last Ice Age.

Like other species, however, the Sumatran rhino has suffered at the hands of humans. Once widespread throughout much of southeast Asia, these shy, rainforest dwellers declined quickly during the last century due to heavy poaching. By the late 1970s, no more than 2,000 remained. By the early 1990s, the number was down to around 300. Even worse, these survivors were in small populations scattered throughout Indonesia and Malaysia, with no more than a few dozen animals in each location. "We now suspect that some of these populations are doomed," says Nico van Strien, a member of the International Rhino Foundation who has studied Sumatran rhinos since 1975.

A somewhat alien-like appearance adds to the mystique of the rarely seen Sumatran rhino.

Conservationists have taken desperate measures. In 1984, they made the controversial decision to capture 40 Sumatran rhinos and transfer them to zoos around the world. The goal was to encourage reproduction in captivity and generate offspring that could be used as insurance against extinction in the wild.

> But the expensive project was a disappointment, with many of the animals dying almost immediately after arriving at their new homes. Researchers knew little about the breeding habits of these shy creatures, and 17 years passed before the first successful birth—a calf named Andalas, born at the Cincinnati Zoo on September 13, 2001. This was followed by the birth of a second calf at the same zoo in 2004.

The Sumatran rhino's unusual hairy hide is a reminder of its prehistoric cousin, the long extinct woolly rhinceros.

Happy as these events were, they are hardly the insurance that conservationists had in mind. Indeed, by the time Andalas was born van Strien and others were already working on Plan B, a network of Sumatran rhino sanctuaries. These are fenced-in areas within natural habitat, where scientists hope the animals will feel at home, and thus more likely to reproduce more frequently. Since the late 1990s, they've built three sanctuaries but they've yet to witness a successful birth. Indeed, the project suffered a severe setback in November 2003, when disease killed all five rhinos at a sanctuary in Malaysia.

As a result, survival of the species continues to depend on the watchful eyes of the Rhino Protection Units (RPUs). The units were established in 1995, when authorities realized that poachers were killing rhinos without any fear of being seen, let alone being thrown in jail. This is because Sumatran rhinos are notoriously shy. They inhabit remote corners of national parks where game wardens rarely visit. Poachers were regularly venturing into these remote areas to set leg snares and other traps. "It was obvious we needed to get people into the rhino area as a first line of defense," recalls van Strien. "The animals needed protection."

∧ Escaping the sweltering tropical heat, a Sumatran rhino wallows in a muddy watering hole.

The teams, which consist of four or five people, take turns scouring the forest for signs of poachers. They also destroy traps and snares, arrest intruders, collect information on how poaching networks operate and spend time talking to local villagers about the importance of conservation.

So far the strategy is working. In one park, for instance, RPUs destroyed 67 traps or snares in the first six months of 1998. Two years later they were no longer finding any. In all the areas where RPUs operate, only three rhinos are known to have been lost since the program began. "As soon as an RPU establishes in an area," says van Strien, "poaching basically stops."

Because of this, the Sumatran rhino's dramatic decline appears to have been halted. Indeed, the teams are now seeing evidence of calves, raising the possibility that at least some populations may be growing. The species is a long way from being out of danger—any recovery will take decades. Still, for the world's most beleaguered rhino, there's now a ray of hope.

BABY ON BOARD

On the morning of September 13, 2001, Terri Roth was filled with excitement. The director of the Cincinnati Zoo's Center for Conservation and Research of Endangered Wildlife had been up all night monitoring Emi, a 1,800-pound (815 kg) Sumatran rhino that was about to deliver a calf after nearly 16 months of pregnancy. Only one other Sumatran rhino had ever given birth successfully in captivity, and that had been 112 years earlier.

> "My big worry was that the calf would be born dead," she recalls. "So the biggest relief came before it was even all the way out, when I saw its front legs kicking. That told me he was alive."

The birth was an opportunity for scientists like Roth to learn more about an essential part of any conservation effort—reproduction. This is especially important for rhinos because they are extremely slow breeders. Females (called cows) do not reach sexual maturity for four to seven years, while males take even longer. When a rhino does get pregnant, she carries the fetus for up to a year and a half, longer than any land mammal except the African elephant. And once the calf is born it may be three or four years before the mother gives birth again. This means a rhino cow might have just eight or nine calves during a 40-year life span.

> This timetable means that even under perfect conditions, no group of rhinos can bounce back quickly. Experts are normally thrilled if a population expands by 10 percent in a given year, and conditions are rarely perfect.

Fortunately, conservationists have some strategies for helping rhino populations rebound. These include both relocating animals from healthy populations to other areas and captive breeding, either in zoos or in large enclosures built around natural habitat. Of course, what all populations need is time. "It takes a great deal of patience and perseverance," says Roth. "Rhinos simply can't rebound overnight."

< Efforts to rear rare Sumatran rhinos in captivity were buoyed by Emi and her second calf, born at the Cincinnati Zoo in 2004.

For several months in 2002, researchers combed Ujung Kulon National Park looking for signs of Javan rhinos. As always, it was no easy task. The park, on the western tip of the Indonesian island of Java, is filled with dense rainforest unfriendly to any large mammal not wearing a thick hide. On top of this, the rhinos are active mainly at night, making them next to impossible to find.

To overcome these obstacles, researchers looked for footprints, collected dung samples and set up "camera traps" designed to snap photos of passing animals. The results indicated a population of 50 to 60 rhinos, including four calves.

∧ Javan rhinos are the world's rarest rhinos.

If this seems like a doctor watching over a critically ill patient, that's about right. The Ujung Kulon rhinos are the last viable population of the world's rarest rhinos. The only Javan rhinos known to live elsewhere were discovered in 1988 in Vietnam, and this small group appears to be dying out. So the species' hopes now rest entirely on the Javan population. Conservationists are doing everything they can to help it grow, and they hope to someday establish a second group. "Ideally, more than one population is required for a species' survival," says Adhi Hariyadi, head of Project Ujung Kulon National Park. "Should anything happen to one of the populations—disease, catastrophe, habitat destruction—then we would have a backup."

To study the elusive Javan rhino, conservationists turn to camera traps hidden deep in the animal's rainforest habitat.

Certainly Ujung Kulon knows catastrophe. It's just 30 miles (50 km) from Krakatoa, an island that exploded in 1883 in one of the greatest volcanic eruptions in history. The blast triggered tsunamis, giant waves more than 120 feet (40 m) high that demolished villages and large swaths of forest, killing some 36,000 people. In the aftermath, Ujung Kulon was no place for humans, and in 1921 it was set aside as a nature reserve.

For the Javan rhino, this was good luck indeed. Once common throughout Southeast Asia, the species was being gradually displaced by humans even before Krakatoa blew its lid. Poachers were still a threat, though, until the early 1960s, when World Wildlife Fund made the Javan rhino one of its first projects. At that time the population was down to 20 or 30 animals, but anti-poaching patrols seemed to produce immediate results. By the 1980s, the number of Javan rhinos had more than doubled.

51

Unfortunately, since then the population has not grown even though poaching has been kept at bay, and conservationists are not sure why. The park is small—not even one-tenth the size of Yellowstone National Park—but it should be able to hold at least 80 rhinos.

One factor is a fast-growing plant called langkap, a member of the palm family whose broad, shade-producing leaves may prevent the growth of some smaller plants that Javan rhinos like to eat.

Another problem might be Ujung Kulon's population of banteng, a type of wild cattle. These animals normally prefer to feed in grassy areas surrounding the park, but as their numbers have grown in recent years, they've moved into areas inhabited by rhinos. Conservationists wonder whether there may not be enough room for so many large mammals. "The banteng are taking up space, which limits the size of the rhinos' home ranges," says Hariyadi. "This may be limiting the rhinos' access to food and wallowing holes."

To test this idea, scientists would like to see what would happen if they moved banteng to other areas, or if additional grassland was created outside the park to lure these competitors away.

∧ Banteng, wild cattle native to Indonesia, may be crowding out the endangered Javan rhino.

Wildlife biologist Adhi Hariyadi tracks the rarest of the rhinos.

Teams continue to keep a careful eye on the remaining Javan rhinos. The four newborn rhinos found in 2002, along with four others discovered two years earlier, is proof that the rhinos are breeding. But this only adds to the mystery of why the population isn't growing. "We still have much to learn," says Hariyadi. "We roughly know the birth rate of the animals, but we do not know the mortality rate."

The trick now will be to find out—before it's too late.

In the mid-1990s Sushila Nepali went on a mission to convince villagers living near Nepal's national parks that conservation was a good thing.

∧ Sushila Nepali, left, has dedicated her career to saving Indian rhinos and their habitat.

Her job was difficult. Since wilderness areas were first set aside in the mid-1970s, they've been viewed as nothing but trouble by many who live near them. Nepal is one of the world's poorest countries, and villagers are not allowed to enter the parks to gather wood, grass and other resources they need to live. If their crops were damaged by rhinos or other wildlife, they were out of luck. When the government finally decided to help, few people were willing to listen. "When we organized meetings," recalls Nepali, "nobody would come."

But Nepali didn't give up. Working first for the Nepalese government and more recently for World Wildlife Fund, she has spent more than six years going door to door and village to village. Along the way she's managed to convince many skeptical villagers that protecting habitat can be good for humans as well as animals.

One of her most important achievements has been forming local committees and helping them think up ways to generate money without destroying the forests. So far Nepali has helped 37 communities form such groups, and their activities have included tree farming, tourism and sustainable grass harvesting.

She's also helping humans and wildlife live side by side. Farmers have learned to protect their crops from rhinos and other animals by digging trenches, putting up fences or erecting watch towers. They're being encouraged to grow mint, lemongrass and other crops that animals don't like to eat. And villagers are being paid by the government if wildlife damages their property.

For Nepali, who was born and raised in the capital city of Kathmandu, the work has meant a life living in grass huts with no electricity or running water. But it's a sacrifice she's willing to make, and she's encouraged by the great gains that have already been made. "If people are not a part of conservation," she says, "then conservation is not possible."

∧ Nepali's conservation message is now a hit with local villagers, young and old.

WHAT IS THE RHINO'S FUTURE?

These are exciting times for rhino conservationists. The comebacks of the Indian and white rhinos, the return of the black rhino to parts of its former range after decades of slaughter, the success of new ideas like private ownership—these have led to relief where once there was only gloom.

Will it last? In the short term, that depends on whether these efforts continue. Conservationists must keep up their protection of rhinos from poachers, governments and international organizations must continue funding them, and scientists will have to devote research to helping conservationists better understand rhino behavior and biology. In this way, surviving rhinos will thrive and new populations will be established.

Long-term survival, on the other hand, will likely depend on humans finally putting an end to the two major threats that rhinos face: the demand for their horn and the destruction of their habitat. This won't be easy. For thousands of years, humans have been thinking the only good rhino is a dead rhino. It will take decades, perhaps longer, before they're able to see the true value that lies within these magnificent beasts.

But nothing is impossible. A little more than a hundred years ago a great South African hunter felt moved to write about the white rhino: "I cannot think that the species will survive very far into the coming century." Thankfully, he could not have been more mistaken.

56

FAST FACTS

Scientific names • from smallest to largest: Sumatran rhinoceros, *Dicerorhinus sumatrensis* (two subspecies); Javan rhinoceros, *Rhinoceros sondaicus* (two subspecies); black rhinoceros, *Diceros bicornis* (four subspecies); Indian (or greater one-horned) rhinoceros, (*Rhinoceros unicornis*); white rhinoceros, *Ceratotherium simum* (two subspecies)

Size • maximum weight ranges from 2,000 pounds (950 kg) for Sumatran rhinos to 6,000 pounds (2,700 kg) for white rhinos
• maximum height ranges from 5 feet (1.5 m) for the Sumatran rhino to 6.5 feet (2 m) for the Indian rhino
• maximum length ranges from 9.5 feet (2.3 m) for the Sumatran rhino to 15 feet (5 m) for the white rhino

Life span • 35 to 40 years in the wild; close to 50 in captivity

Locomotion • capable of charging at 35 mph (55 kph) over short distances
• Indian and Sumatran rhinos are excellent swimmers

Senses • poor vision, unable to detect a motionless person 100 feet (30 m) away, or to distinguish between a standing person and a tree
• eyes are on either side of the head, so to see forward, the rhino must peer first with one eye, then the other
• relies on keen hearing and smell to detect danger

Communication • uses horn waving, ear wagging and other movements during confrontations over territory or when threatened
• marks territory by spraying urine or building up dung heaps
• uses various grunts, snorts and squeals when threatened or during mating

Diet
- strictly vegetarian
- white rhinos have square-shaped lips for grazing on grass; other rhinos prefer leaves, twigs and branches

Horns
- made from keratin, the same material as hair and fingernails
- used as tools for removing bark or breaking off branches, in defense against lions, tigers or hyenas, and in territorial battles between males
- white, black and Sumatran rhinos have two horns; greater one-horned and Javan rhinos have one
- size ranges from the 10-inch (25 cm) horn of the Javan rhino, to the massive front horn of the white rhino, which can top 5 feet (1.5 m)
- grows at a rate of about 2 inches (5 cm) per year

Teeth
- African rhinos have 24 molars
- Asian rhinos also have tusk-like incisors and, in the case of Sumatran rhinos, lower canines used in fighting

Skin
- thick folds of skin, resembling plates of armor, provide protection from sharp thorns and branches
- leathery skin of the Sumatran rhino is half an inch (1.5 cm) thick and covered with more hair than other species

Reproduction
- gestation lasts 15 to 18 months, depending on the species
- males reach sexual maturity between seven and 10 years of age, females between four and seven
- one calf born every three to four years

HOW YOU CAN HELP

For more information about rhinos and the projects designed to save them, contact the following:

International Rhino Foundation
www.rhinos-irf.org

White Oak Conservation Center
3823 Owens Road, Yulee, FL U.S.A. 32097
Founded in 1989, the IRF is one of the leading groups dedicated entirely to rhino conservation.

Save the Rhino International
www.savetherhino.org

16 Winchester Walk, London SE1 9AQ United Kingdom
Phone +44 (0)20 7357 7474
Founded in 1991, SRI raises funds for conservation by hosting Rhino Adventures, in which participants run marathons and other races.

SOS Rhino
www.sosrhino.org

680 N. Lake Shore Drive, Suite 807, Chicago, IL U.S.A. 60611
Phone (312) 222-0440
Funds research and other conservation projects, with a focus on a rare subspecies of Sumatran rhino found on the island of Borneo.

World Wildlife Fund US
www.worldwildlife.org

1250 24th Street NW, P.O. Box 97180, Washington, DC U.S.A. 20090-7180
Phone (800) 225-5993
Has an excellent Web site that outlines its rhino conservation efforts and provides entertaining ways to learn more.

Bowling for Rhinos
www.bfr.aazk.org

An annual bowl-a-thon that involves groups throughout Canada and the United States, raising money for rhino conservation in Kenya and Indonesia. Check the Web site for info on how you can organize your own fundraiser.

The IUCN African Rhino Specialist Group
www.iucn.org

KwaZulu-Natal Nature Conservation Service
PO Box 13053, Cascades 3202 South Africa
The World Conservation Union's organization dedicated to white and black rhinos.

The IUCN Asian Rhino Specialist Group
www.iucn.org

No. 10 Jalan Bomoh, Off Jalan Keramat Hujong, 54200 Kuala Lumpur, Malaysia
The World Conservation Union's organization devoted to the Javan, Sumatran and Indian rhinos.

INDEX

PHOTO CREDITS

AUTHOR'S NOTE

Rhino conservationists are busy people. Many thanks to those experts who set aside time from their hectic schedules to talk about their work, particularly Rob Brett, Martin Brooks, Eric Dinerstein, Richard Emslie, Jacques Flamand, Adhi Hariyadi, Eugene Lee, Esmond Martin, Sushila Nepali, Lee Poston, Terri Roth, Nico van Strien, Rob Slotow and Bibhab Talukdar.

This book is for Will.